THE RESPONSIBILITIES OF BUSINESS LEADERSHIP

LONDON : GEOFFREY CUMBERLEGE
OXFORD UNIVERSITY PRESS

The Responsibilities of Business Leadership

EDITED BY

Harwood F. Merrill

EDITOR, MODERN INDUSTRY
PRESIDENT, HARVARD BUSINESS SCHOOL
ALUMNI ASSOCIATION

HARVARD UNIVERSITY PRESS

Cambridge, Massachusetts

1948

PRINTED IN THE UNITED STATES OF AMERICA

FOREWORD

Every day we hear more of the need for business and the men who manage business to live up to their responsibilities. It is generally conceded that the first responsibility of a businessman is to be a competent businessman — one who knows how to run his job and make a profit. But when you ask what his further responsibilities are, you get in reply only vague generalities. And who can head for a destination without some sort of map or chart to guide him?

We are providing such a map in this book, by defining the responsibilities of the businessman to each of the many groups that are affected by his activities — the public, workers, the government; and consumers, stockholders, and the world beyond our borders. The articles are based on speeches the authors made at the Eighteenth Annual Conference of the Harvard Business School Alumni Association at Soldiers Field, Boston, June 12, 1948. The Introduction by Dean David is adapted from remarks he made before the Harvard Business School Club of New York on May 17, 1948.

The men who treat the six major areas of business responsibility in this book are exceptionally well qualified to do so. They have not only thought deeply about the subject with which each is concerned; but also have actually put into successful practice the principles they offer.

There was a time when the sole responsibility of the businessman was considered to be (in the few instances when it was considered at all) to make money. This was principally a responsibility to himself and to a small group of others associated with him. And so business and the businessman could live to themselves.

But that idea has long since vanished, and one much more appropriate to the complicated and challenging world of 1948 has taken its place. This new concept is, of course, that the businessman's responsibilities extend far beyond himself and his immediate associates; that the chief ones, in fact, are to others, to the many groups on which his decisions and actions have some sort of impact.

The very success of the businessman has created these new responsibilities for him. He has thoroughly earned his place as the most important single influence in the economic and social well-being of this nation. But because of that same fact, he has inevitably been the focal point of responsibilities in keeping with the importance of his place.

If he refuses to accept these responsibilities, then they certainly will be taken over by someone else — by someone antagonistic to business management and to free enterprise, the only system under which business management can operate. The challenge to the men who manage business is just as simple as that. Either businessmen accept their responsibilities — or those responsibilities will pass to some other group, and businessmen and free enterprise will move out of the picture.

Against that background, what these men say should furnish food for thought for a long time to come. It should furnish food for action, too, though at first sight the extent of the businessman's responsibilities may seem frightening. It looks as if he needs to know so much and to do so much, that it is impossible for any human being to reach the goal.

But one relatively simple thought can come to our rescue at this point and put matters in proper perspective. The many ideas presented in this book boil down, in the end, to one: that if one acts toward others as he would want them to act toward him, then he will be on the right road toward discharging his business responsibilities. That, of course, is only a restatement of the golden rule. There is nothing new in it. But it is a truth that is as vitally important today as when it was first stated. And it is the one rule of the road that can lead businessmen out of the wilderness. Our responsibilities look less overwhelming when we think of them in that light.

So let's do something about these responsibilities ourselves. Let's not leave it up to the other fellow.

Eugene Holman, president of Standard Oil Company (N.J.), has expressed this idea precisely. He said, recently:

> *Clearly, there is a price tag on human liberty. That price is the willingness to assume the responsibilities of being free men.*

Payment of this price is a personal matter with each of us. It is not something that we can get others to pay for us. To let others carry the responsibilities of freedom, and the work and worry that accompany them — while we share only in the benefits — may be a very human impulse, but it is likely to be fatal.

I commend that thought to every businessman.

HARWOOD F. MERRILL

August 2, 1948

CONTENTS

Introduction xi
Donald Kirk David
Dean of the Harvard Graduate School of Business Administration

Businessmen's Responsibilities to the Public 1
Clarence Francis
Chairman of the Board, General Foods Corporation

Businessmen's Responsibilities to Employees 15
Richard R. Deupree
President, The Procter & Gamble Company

Businessmen's Responsibilities to Government 27
Ralph E. Flanders
United States Senator from Vermont

Businessmen's Responsibilities to Consumers 41
Jack I. Straus
President, R. H. Macy and Company, Inc.

Businessmen's Responsibilities to Stockholders 57
Harry A. Bullis
Chairman of the Board, General Mills, Inc.

Businessmen's Responsibilities to the World 73
Allen W. Dulles
Partner, Sullivan and Cromwell

INTRODUCTION

DONALD KIRK DAVID

We in North America live in an industrial civilization. Business is essential to our lives; business determines our material welfare and has an important influence on our emotional welfare. We have grown into the habit of looking forward to an increasing standard of living as well as a continuing place in world trade. In such a society, therefore, business leadership cannot help but be of great importance to the course which our civilization takes. By the very nature of the system, the businessman has especially heavy responsibilities. He must understand them; he must be prepared to meet them. To me the brightest ray of hope in these troubled times is my firm belief that the businessman can and will measure up to the task. It is not easy; we have a great deal to learn; but it can be done.

The task of business leadership involves making decisions and accepting responsibility. No good administrator or executive lacks this instinctive acceptance of responsibility — responsibility not only toward his company and industry but also toward the community, the nation, and even the world. He must test in the light of the broader public interest his own actions, the actions of his company, and the actions of the business world at large. He must realize that powerful forces result from the collective actions of such businessmen as he, just as the collective actions of workers and farmers create other powerful forces. The businessman, however, is the main source of initiative in our economy and his position is one of unusual influence; his responsibilities are correspondingly great. The businessman therefore does what he can to strengthen the social structure of his community, local or national.

The alert businessman seeks to understand the economic, social, and political forces which shape the environment within which he operates. He recognizes that there are weaknesses and deficiencies in this structure. He knows that freedom of enterprise is a dynamic and therefore, almost by definition, a changing concept. With his understanding of the climate in which business operates, with his appreciation of the historical foundations of our system and its current and evolving functions, the competent businessman will strive continually toward improvement in the social and economic structure itself. This is not only his duty as a businessman, but also his obligation as a citizen and as a leader in the community.

Of course it is not difficult to find evidence that at times some businessmen have put greedy gain ahead of what the Constitution calls the "general welfare." Such actions are not defensible, but all types of leadership are guilty at times of similar offenses. And the plain simple fact is that our system has worked pretty well.

We have a higher standard of material welfare than

any other nation in history; we have developed and maintained noticeably higher degrees of personal freedom — and for more of our people — than have existed in most of the societies that the world now knows or has known.

We accept change in our society — perhaps more willingly than most societies. Our society is dynamic. In this lies its strength. Its good points can be retained; its bad ones eliminated. It can be adjusted to new conditions, without being destroyed.

In the eyes of some impatient critics the very strength of our society is a weakness. We are in truth a society composed of millions of centers of initiative. Almost every citizen, and literally every businessman, day after day, makes decisions which shape our society. It is not planned neatly and completely at the top; its planning is done at all levels from bottom upwards. A complex system and one difficult to understand, but it works. And it has given us something that few people have ever had — freedom of opportunity. And, in turn, this freedom of opportunity is our greatest potential asset in the conflict with the totalitarians. This means that the leadership of our society as a whole can be continuously reinforced and revitalized by recruits from all segments of our population. Providing places for talent thus developed requires a dynamic, risk-taking, and venturesome setting. No rigidly limited and confined party membership narrowly defines the source from which our leadership may come. No single center of initiative controls our destiny.

To my mind, the way to make our system work better is perfectly clear. The system cannot be improved by superimposing all-pervasive planning at the top; that does not improve the system — it changes it. The way to do it is to improve the quality of the decisions all along the line. Let them be made where they are now; but improve their quality by increasing the consciousness of the responsibility which accompanies each decision.

This consciousness of responsibility means that the businessman must direct his efforts toward certain purposes, certain ideals. He must have in mind constantly the values which he seeks. As I see it, there are two major objectives toward which the administrative capacities and attitudes of the ideal businessman should be directed.

As a first objective, the competent business administrator must furnish society with material satisfactions. To do this, he must be a maker of jobs and therefore a maker of profits. In thinking of profits he must not be a slave to the annual financial statement but must take the longer view. The competent business administrator must know that in a free society his enterprise can maintain profits over any considerable period of time only by serving the public and by achieving a proper balance among the real long-term interests of employees, stockholders, suppliers, customers, and all others directly affected by the activities of the business. Upon the competence with which these interests are balanced and these functions performed rests the possibility of continuously raising the material standard of living of our people. Under our system, only the business which makes a profit makes a contribution. For a time a business that does not make a profit can continue in existence, but only because it is subsidized by other parts of society. Over the longer period it cannot be a good producer of material satisfactions or even a good taxpayer; in the long run, it becomes a drain on society.

The second objective which the competent business administrator must recognize and willingly accept is an even greater responsibility. We all know that the material standard of living, the physical satisfactions of life, are very far from the whole story. I maintain that in an industrial civilization business leaders must assume the responsibility for increasing all the human satisfactions of the group with which they are associated.

The problem of responsible business leadership has been well summarized by President Conant:

> As never before, business needs men who appreciate the responsibilities of business to itself and to that unique society of free men which has been developed on this continent. Such men must understand not only the practical workings of business organizations, but also the economic and social climate in which business operates; they must be as well trained as our professional men in law and medicine.

Happily there is developing on this continent an outstanding and growing group of business managers who recognize the responsibility of business leadership and who are devoting funds and effort to study how best to meet this responsibility.

BUSINESSMEN'S RESPONSIBILITIES TO THE PUBLIC

BY

Clarence Francis

CHAIRMAN OF THE BOARD
GENERAL FOODS CORPORATION
NEW YORK, NEW YORK

Clarence Francis, chairman of the board of General Foods Corporation, is an able practitioner of what he advocates. His company's and his own activities serve as good examples of his subject: What businessmen need to do to meet their responsibilities to the public — that is, to the businessman's community, whether it is a town, a state, or the whole nation . . . Mr. Francis started in the food business as a sales clerk. He has been in it ever since, moving from Corn Products Refining Company to Ralston Purina, and then, in 1924, to General Foods. He became president in 1935 and chairman of the board in 1943 . . . Mr. Francis has been active in the affairs of his home community, Bronxville, New York, and has devoted a good deal of time to serving our national government. Among other government assignments, he has been chairman of the Food Industry War Committee; chief industrial consultant, Defense Plants Corporation; and member of the Business Advisory Council of the United States Department of Commerce. He is also a director, among other companies, of Air Reduction, Chemical Bank and Trust Company, and Northern Pacific Railroad.

BUSINESSMEN'S RESPONSIBILITIES TO THE PUBLIC

This program is, to me, truly significant. Within my memory there was a time when neither audience nor speakers could have been found to consider the responsibilities of business leadership in quite the terms in which we view them now. Today there are schools to teach business administration, as Harvard does so well. There is a body of knowledge to be taught. There are businessmen who can speak from experience of the ways in which business can and does meet responsibility.

But this program is significant for another reason. Business is just one element of our complex political economy. Yet I wonder how often civil servants — or trade unionists, or lawyers, or physicians, or even clergymen — hold meetings solely for the purpose of discussing their responsibilities. Why, then, do we? Is it because we are especially conscientious? I wish I could think so. Actually, I believe it is because our calling is so new, because our task is so vital, and because we are, frankly, a bit bewildered.

America's industrial power has developed, after all, in a few generations. The patterns of human leadership, on the other hand, are usually centuries in the making. To put it another way, we know that it takes as long to select and train pilots for the responsibility of flying as it does to build planes. Yet fate has forced management to take the controls of our high-powered, delicate economic mechanism — with little formal preparation and with no choice but to fly. Technically and mechanically our progress has been dazzling. In the area of human relationships, however, we have had to fly by the stars.

Consider definitions for a moment. "Management" as a noun applied to a group of men is almost as new as next week's slang. "Business leadership" is a phrase so challenging that we could spend hours in a search for its meaning. "Responsibility" and "public," however, are among the oldest words we know. They have been available to leaders in every field for centuries. We may take some comfort, perhaps, from asking if there is a single human institution that has ever met all of its public responsibilities. I doubt it — for institutions *are* human.

This fact will not excuse us, however, from making every effort to perfect ourselves in our work. The pressures are great and there is much at stake. People seem to realize instinctively that modern industry is directly related to human welfare socially and politically in every area. There is no longer any debate as to whether there shall, or shall not, be industry. Nazi Germany had industry. Russia has industry. Other nations want industry. The question before the world is how industry shall be run, for what purpose, and by whom.

We represent the free American system. We believe it to be superior to any totalitarian system. But it is up to us to demonstrate this fact. How do we go about this? To get the true answer we must first seek *motives* rather than methods, *principles* rather than procedures. This is a questioning age and we must begin by questioning ourselves. Why, for example, does Mr. Deupree speak of responsibilities to workers? Why does Mr. Straus speak of responsibilities to consumers? Why does Mr. Bullis speak of stockholders, Senator Flanders of government, and Mr. Dulles of the world?

The answer is important, I think. The answer is that here are men who have the *will* to define and meet responsibilities. This means to me that real progress has been made. This means to me that the pilots of the industrial mechanism are developing instruments by which to chart a more exact course in the stratosphere of human relations. But first, remember, they had to *want* to do so.

Now let us take a glance backward, which will help us to measure the progress of which I speak. In the past century much of industry's great growth was achieved by men whose motives sometimes bordered on the primitive. In the mid-Nineteenth Century, the pioneers of the machine age swept across the continent transforming a wealth of raw materials into a wealth of new devices. Let us never underestimate those men. It may truly be said of many of them that "There were giants in those days." They made great contributions to our national development. Profit was, however, their main, if not their only, motive. Some of them brought upon themselves and upon business generally, a storm of public indignation from which we still suffer today. Many were denounced as "robber barons," "malefactors of great wealth," "exploiters," "freebooters," and all the rest. The era of "laissez-faire" was followed quickly by a public demand for curbs and regulations upon unbridled individualism. From this it became apparent that the profit motive alone was not good enough to justify free business operation.

Now, somewhere along the line, since the days of the early monopolists, several important changes have taken place in the attitude of business leadership. Perhaps catch phrases denote mileposts. In that case it is interesting to suppose that William H. Vanderbilt may have been expressing a new point of view when he said "The public be damned." This, as it happened, drew down upon him a torrent of public abuse. Actually few people heard the rest of what he said. The phrase was inadvertently spoken when someone asked Vanderbilt why the New York Central was withdrawing an extra-fare train. And what he really said was this: "The public be damned — I am working for my stockholders. If the public want the train, why don't they pay for it?" This was much different from something his father, Commodore Cornelius Vanderbilt, had said years before. For, speaking in the spirit of his own times, the elder Vanderbilt once declared: "What do I care about the law — ain't I got the power?"

As a matter of fact, William H. Vanderbilt took the lead in broadening the ownership of his enterprises to include large numbers of new stockholders.

He considered it a mistake for so much power to be vested in one man. This may have marked a trend. At any rate, we have since seen the inclusion of more and more people as business participants. Today millions of stockholders have a personal stake in industry.

It was next to be learned, however, that the service of the stockholder is not in itself a sufficient motive for the operation of business. New indignations were voiced — this time by consumers condemning shoddy and fraudulent claims. Again regulatory intervention occurred. New millions gained an acknowledged voice in the operation of industry.

Then more millions asserted still another claim. Employees banded together to demand consideration of their services as something more than a commodity. Again clashes occurred and public opinion finally expressed itself in support of the workers' claims. Today the rights of employee organizations have been so fully recognized in law that they have had to be redefined — by law.

Finally, we have learned, during two great wars, that government, in emergencies, can exert a claim on industry's energies that transcends all other claims.

I realize that I am oversimplifying a complex story. Most of these developments did not come into clear focus at exact times. They did not necessarily follow in order. They are still evolving.

But, I repeat, *progress has been made.* Speaking personally, I do not know a single businessman of any consequence today who would engage in some of the trade practices and labor policies that were a comparative commonplace fifty years ago. No member of my board of directors would condone a shady or dishonest policy on the part of our management. And this is not to confer unsolicited halos on my associates. I think this attitude is quite general. Today, most managements, in fact, operate as trustees in recognition of the claims of employees, investors, consumers, and government. The task is to keep these forces in balance and to see that each gets a fair share of industry's rewards. We have seen the general acceptance of a series of "Thou Shalt Nots." No Moses brought them down from a mountaintop. It simply came to be generally agreed that "Honesty is the best policy."

But, having accepted the "Do Nots," are we not ready now for an era of positive "Do's"? The Decalogue, after all, did no more than impose certain necessary restrictions on human conduct. A new era began when the Sermon on the Mount opened mankind's eyes to the possibilities of affirmative good will. I am not ashamed to predict to you that the next age of business leadership will belong to those who count their success in terms of the greatest possible service to the greatest number of people. I say that the human problems of industry are the big problems and that they will not yield to techniques alone—important as these may be.

There must be at bottom a *will* to make business work in the public interest. And preceding that there must be an agreement on *motives*. Can anyone forget the miraculous unanimity with which Americans came together in wartime? We were agreed on the *reasons why.*

Let us now study our own motives as businessmen. Are our reasons why good enough for the future? Why do we get up in the morning and hurry to work? To hold a job? To make a sale? To finish a blueprint? To balance a set of figures? Those are worthy aims — but they are not sufficient as ends in themselves. Very well: We work for our families, to educate our children, to acquire comforts, leisure, and security. Worthier by far — but still not good enough. I believe we are working for freedom, just as we fought for freedom. I believe we are making a system work because without it neither we nor others can be free. I believe we are proving every day to the world that the American way of operating industry is the best way.

This is not to say that we have perfected our system — far from it. Perhaps we should admit that the system itself is vastly better than the mere men who run it, just as the ideal of democracy is vastly better than any performance that its human practitioners have given to date.

The principle of free enterprise is one we can and must defend vigorously while admitting its imperfections. It is the essence of individual liberty. For when the state owns enterprise, it assumes control over the individual's livelihood — and man inevitably becomes the political and social as well as the economic servant of the state.

On the positive side, there is another way of proving the worth of our system. We must produce, build, expand, and pour forth goods in abundance — not only for the nation but for the world. In that way we can spread both freedom and wealth until, God willing, there need be no war.

Are those goals good enough? If so, we have the *motives* we need to do the job ahead of us. I wonder if there is not some way in which young men can be dedicated to management with a full sense of the human importance of their tasks. Perhaps a sort of Hippocratic Oath could be devised to remind us of the moral responsibilities of true business leadership. If we were to formulate a pledge to govern all management — young men starting out, junior executives, and department heads as well as top executives — it might run something like this:

I believe that a business must be run at an adequate profit and must hold its own in fair competition with other businesses

. . . within my sphere I will do my best to help keep my business prosperous and strong.

I believe that business must serve employees, stockholders, consumers, and government and that management must keep the interests of all these elements in balance

. . . to the extent of my authority I will try to preserve this balance.

I believe that management's operating goals are continuously improved productivity and growth, in order to provide jobs, reward investors, attract capital, and provide more and better goods and services at lower cost

. . . in any capacity in which I find myself I will work toward those goals.

I believe further that the greatest assets of a business are its human assets and that the improvement of their value is both a matter of material advantage and moral obligation; I believe, therefore, that employees must be treated as honorable individuals, justly rewarded, encouraged in their progress, fully informed, and properly assigned, and that their lives and work must be given meaning and dignity, on and off the job

. . . if I have the supervision of so much as one other person I will strive to honor these principles in practice.

I believe that a reputation for integrity is another priceless asset of any business and that management must deal fairly with customers, competitors, and vendors, advertise truthfully, fulfill its commitments, coöperate with other managements in the betterment of business as a whole, and oppose any artificial restriction that may limit production, fix prices, or restrain trade

. . . in my daily work I will try to deserve, and make my business deserve, a reputation for integrity.

I believe that the future of the American economic system depends on the confidence, good will, and understanding of the people and that business leadership must make itself a responsible part of the human community by participating in worthy activities locally and nationally

. . . as a representative of business and as an individual I will identify my business and myself with the welfare of people.

I believe that whenever business has earned a hearing, it has not only a right but a duty to ask for public confidence and that it must speak freely, give information gladly, and answer the attacks of those who seek to undermine American freedom under democratic capitalism

. . . I will speak out in behalf of my business and the system which it represents.

I believe, finally, that business leadership is nothing less than a public trust, that it must offer a message of courage and hope to all people, and that it can help an economically strong America to lead other nations to lasting prosperity, freedom, and peace

. . . I will work not only for the advancement of myself, my family, and my country but for liberty and democracy for America and for the world — now and in the years to come.

That is not a perfect code, I know; but it does constitute a statement of objectives that seems to me worthy of our every effort. Perhaps no one of us is humanly capable of living up to all these principles. Yet I shall always believe that it is far better to fall short of a high standard than to accept and live by a low one. Moreover, I don't think the public demands or expects perfection of us. People simply want to know that leadership is conscious of, and trying to meet, responsibility.

To be realistic, I am sure that complete acceptance

of these principles would not solve all the problems of administration and human relationships, and we will always make mistakes. I have often said that I am glad there is no one person who knows of all of my mistakes; I should hate to see a convention of all of the people who know of some of them.

But I repeat once again: *Progress has been made* — and boundless progress lies before us if we have faith in the rightness of that which we do.

Sometimes I think we might humanly be justified in resting on our laurels a bit. The economic greatness of free America is an actual fact. The promises of its totalitarian critics are nine-tenths fantasy. Surely business must have met some of its responsibilities or our living standards would not be so high. But we cannot yield to complacency for one moment. No matter how great our achievements, we must keep our eyes on the greater goals ahead. The millions on whose verdict the final fate of our business system will depend are interested *not* in yesterday's triumphs but in tomorrow's promise.

If we pause for long we can hear a rumble of denunciation from a hostile Left. If we listen closely we can hear echoes of cynicism and despair on every hand. We ourselves can fall prey to cynicism, for we meet frequently with discouragement. The temptation to compromise our principles often appears in inviting forms.

In a manner that appeals greatly to me, Raymond B. Fosdick* recently restated our national objectives.

* *New York Times Magazine,* June 6, 1948.

We need not dollars alone but faith, he declared, reminding us that we were born in a revolution that

> sprang from a passionate belief in freedom and in the worth and dignity and creative capacity of the human individual.
>
> This is the tradition of America [he warns], and we must not let the song die on our lips. The foundations of this country were based on moral principles that emphasized the rights of men everywhere to all that makes life satisfying and rewarding . . . Our faith once captured the imagination of the world; it can capture it again.

Let us reject cynicism in all its forms and accept the challenge of tomorrow. Within and beyond our borders, it is in the realm of moral principle that the real responsibility of businessmen will be discharged. The test of leadership is its capacity to lead. We know the principles to be sound. We need the faith and the will to make them work.

MANAGEMENT'S RESPONSIBILITIES TO EMPLOYEES

BY

Richard R. Deupree

PRESIDENT
THE PROCTER & GAMBLE COMPANY
CINCINNATI, OHIO

The businessman's responsibilities to workers is an area that has been almost continually in the news for the past fifteen years. It is perhaps the most discussed of all business responsibilities. It is certainly one of the most important, and one with which the businessman has to wrestle practically every day of the year . . . It is particularly appropriate that this subject has been covered by Richard R. Deupree, president of the Procter & Gamble Company. Few companies have gone as far as Procter & Gamble in meeting their responsibilities to workers. And since Mr. Deupree has been an officer of the company since 1924, and its president since 1930, one can make an assumption which fits the facts: His leadership, and Procter & Gamble's progressive industrial-relations policies, are mostly a case of cause and effect . . . Besides being a director of many other companies in addition to the one he heads, Mr. Deupree has found time to serve his home community and the national government in many capacities, including that of the executive chairmanship of the Army-Navy Munitions Board. He is also a member of the Visiting Committee of the Harvard Business School.

MANAGEMENT'S RESPONSIBILITIES TO EMPLOYEES

In formulating my thoughts concerning the responsibility of management to the employee, I constantly found myself working toward an ideal relationship. You might call it a "business utopia," this ideal relationship between employer and employee. You might see no similarity between it and today's business headlines, or yesterday's, or tomorrow's. Nevertheless, events are moving in this direction — business has made remarkable progress the last several years.

A clear-thinking, understanding management that is interested in, and knows, the employees and their problems has certain responsibilities. My idea is to give you the five points which I consider to be of primary importance. Briefly, these goals of management's responsibilities to employees are: (1) a successful business — one that earns regular profits; (2) steady employment; (3) the opportunity of the individual employee to develop to the fullest extent of his abilities; (4) the employee's chance to become a capitalist; (5) good working conditions.

Now I'll admit that these objectives have never been reached completely by any one employer, though a great number of companies have taken important steps in this direction. Gains have been made and are constantly being made toward realizing these responsibilities of management. The first step is management's recognition of the problems of labor: studying the causes and effects in helping to solve those problems. The newer labor leaders must realize their responsibilities, too; they represent a new kind of management on a gigantic scale in their unions.

We have passed through fifteen of the most difficult years in the history of this nation. No one can doubt that labor has made more gains in those fifteen years than were made in any previous period of three times fifteen.

Today the great difficulty, as you and I know, is to have a sensible meeting of minds between employers and employees on a realistic basis to solve problems in a sane, fair, and equitable way. This is a very, very difficult thing to do with certain situations as they exist in some industries in this country today — but, again I say, real progress is being made.

Some firms, like Procter & Gamble, have labored for years to work out reasonable and satisfactory relations with employees. Others have not had those years of experience. Some men in our company have spent almost their entire business lives working on that important phase of our business. Some of the groundwork was laid years and years ago. For example, we had a profit-sharing plan for employees in operation as early as 1887. Many other companies have spent years in working out satisfactory relations with their employees. In any organization, it is a slow and gradually evolving process, a process which takes years and, with human nature as it is, one that is never fully completed. With many businesses the groundwork is hardly laid and many years of working toward understanding lie ahead.

Now let me go into some detail and discuss each of my five ideals or goals of management's responsibilities.

To me, the first responsibility of management to its employees is to operate a successful business — a business which makes a profit. I mean a regular, healthy profit, the kind that continues to pay wages and expand a business, thereby making new jobs. It is unfortunate that through the past several years a great many influential people have considered profits as something to be ashamed of and avoided. Never were people more mistaken and misled. Profits are the lifeblood of a business and of the continuing progress of the individuals in the business. There could be no business expansion, no industrial progress, without profits. As for real benefits to employees, just try to find them in a firm which makes no profits. If the condition persists, the "going" business becomes the "gone" business with no jobs.

Employees should realize that, along with profits, the continued financial strength of a company is a managerial responsibility to them. This is particularly important in this period of very high raw material costs, high costs of finished products, and high level of employment.

Good business makes a lot of people say to themselves as they did in the late 1920's, "This is a new-type, never-ending era of prosperity." They go head over heels in debt to build more plant capacity and promote their products to the limit. They haven't thought this business condition through to its logical conclusion. It is all right to borrow money for business needs; it is all right to promote your products; but you had better be dead sure, as sure as man can be, that the business's financial future is not being jeopardized by overexpansion. One must not forget that no matter how long a dry season lasts, it finally ends in rain.

My second point as to the responsibility of management is probably the most important one I have to make, other than that of profits. It is a point that is much harder to get across to management; I know, for I have been talking on this subject for almost twenty years. I refer to a guarantee to the employee of work for a specified number of weeks per year, wherever possible. Our Plan of Guaranteed Employment, which assures eligible employees at least forty-eight weeks' work a year, has been in continuous operation since 1923. Other types of industries have come forward with other plans of stabilized employment; and these plans work.

You will say that stabilized employment is all right for businesses making soap and shortening, or shoes, or processing meats. Let me describe our experience with an industry which was so seasonal that no one believed it could possibly be stabilized. In this branch of our business, the crushing of cottonseed, we had a most serious problem because the amount of our available crushing material was entirely governed by the size of the cotton crop. Ever since cottonseed has been produced for industrial purposes, it has been brought in from the farms to the cottonseed crushing mills, crushed, and the oil moved out during five or six fall and winter months. For this reason, the crushing mills were shut down for six months or so each year, and, of course, the employees were laid off. When we realized that the consumption of products made from that oil — shortening, for instance — went on regularly month after month with slight variations throughout the year, we felt that here, too, something could be done to regulate production to the consumption line. The answer was found in different storage and handling of the seed. Today, our sixteen crushing mills in the South run from ten to twelve months, with a consequent saving in investment for factory capacity per ton of seed and, what is even more surprising, an improved yield and quality of the oil produced from the seed. The steady employment, of course, results in keeping trained men on the job instead of having to train a new crew of men every crop season.

I am not going into further details here but anyone who has given steady, guaranteed employment a fair trial knows its many advantages to the employee and to the company. He's not going back to the old way of up-and-down employment.

With the steady job should come a fair and reasonable wage. The matter of a fair day's pay may be a hard one to define. We have worked it out this way in our business: With our employee representatives we agree upon a list of the better companies in the communities in which we operate plants. Then, through the coöperation of these chosen companies, we obtain and tabulate their basic wage rates for given classifications of jobs. The employee representatives have full access to the figures used in the final calculations. From these calculations we arrive at what we believe is a fair hourly rate for a given job in a given community. The employees know this plan is sensible and fair and it works.

My third point is management's responsibility to give the individual employee a chance to develop the best that is in him. This may sound like a platitude. It is not. Select a man carefully for the job he is going to fill. Give him proper training and supervision. Then give that man a real chance to prove his ability, to earn more money, through a wage incentive plan that pays him for more work produced above the average. If the worker is confident he will be paid according to his ability to produce, you help him and help his production. As he sees himself doing a better job, he gains pride in his work and confidence in himself. The conditions in his home tend to reflect his increased earnings, and you have a much better employee and citizen. Self-respecting employees make the kind of Americans who are eager to serve in their communities.

Naturally such a plan should include a procedure of promotion understood by all. The man who progresses should know where his progress will lead him. Most successful businesses have these plans and have laid down definite procedures. In some, however, promotion is haphazard and employees are likely to feel they haven't a fair chance at the better jobs.

The fourth responsibility of management is that every employee should be helped and given the chance to become a capitalist. This can be done in many ways, and is being done in this country through profit sharing, stock ownership, savings and other plans. Some feel that this objective — that as many employees as possible shall become capitalists — is dreaming. Nevertheless, it has been worked out in our company and many others. The employee, with the help of the company, begins to accumulate capital through stock ownership or a savings plan. He has a bank account; he has financial interest in the company. Pretty soon he is a home owner, and his children are well cared for. That man is a good employee; and when you multiply him by hundreds or thousands, the chance of experiencing trouble in a plant with workers like that is greatly lessened. Workers who own their own homes, have bank accounts, and own stock in their company are the kind of capitalists of which any community can be proud.

The fifth responsibility of management is for proper working conditions. There are many factors to consider under this heading. There is the health of the employee, his safety while at work, and such other general things as recreation facilities, the workday atmosphere of the plant, and the attitude of the other workers. The military services call it *esprit de corps.*

The subject of working conditions is one which tests the mettle of management and employees and their ability to get together, to resolve difficulties. There are a hundred and one problems which come up constantly in a plant — problems that require understanding and proper clarification. Right here let me say that a good decision on working conditions, one good for employees and good for the company, if not properly explained and made clear to employees may lose all of its value and may even cause trouble in the plant. Communications between management and employees are of the utmost importance. We go to great lengths to make clear the reasons for certain decisions and make sure these decisions are understood by employees.

I could dwell on this subject a great deal more; but anyone who has done no more than visit industrial plants can tell how important working conditions can be in affecting the employees' state of mind at work. Two plants side by side can be as different as day and night in the attitude of employees and in the production records of their workers.

There are many other responsibilities of management to employees. Management need not stop with the five I have named. But those I have covered, I believe, are the most important and the most pressing. Let me repeat them briefly: (1) a successful business — one that earns regular profits; (2) steady employment; (3) the opportunity of the individual employee to develop to the fullest extent of his abilities; (4) the employee's chance to become a capitalist; (5) good working conditions.

I think the results of applying these principles are

as apparent as they are valuable for those traveling down the long road to management responsibility. One of the obviously important results is often a greater output per worker, which is one of the main objectives of any producing company. This increased production leads to a lowered cost of goods which I think inevitably means more profits to the company and more benefits to employees. Increased production is the only way I know of to improve the standards of living of our people as a whole and, to my mind, this is a broad responsibility of management to the country at large.

Most important of all, improved working and living conditions for the people of our country represent the strongest possible insurance of the continuance of a free society and our way of life, which has proved its superiority over any other known to mankind.

If management could and would follow through on the five objectives outlined here, I would not worry about any of the "isms" developing in our midst, or outside our country. A man's job, his attitude toward it, and toward the people who work with him, is the core and root of his American citizenship.

BUSINESSMEN'S RESPONSIBILITIES TO GOVERNMENT

BY

Ralph E. Flanders

UNITED STATES SENATOR
FROM VERMONT

Senator Ralph E. Flanders has had a wide-ranging career which includes such varied assignments as machinist apprentice, machine designer, president of Jones and Lamson Machine Company, and president of the National Machine Tool Builders Association and of the American Society of Mechanical Engineers. Now, he is United States Senator from Vermont . . . Business and government have been moving closer together for nearly twenty years, and Senator Flanders, who has seen things from both points of view, is unusually well qualified to discuss the businessman's responsibilities to government. As a senatorial candidate, he won the support of both the Chamber of Commerce and the CIO — which is undoubtedly something new in the senatorial world.

BUSINESSMEN'S RESPONSIBILITIES TO GOVERNMENT

Of course the first responsibility of business to government is to obey the laws, whether those laws are local, state, or federal. I am assuming that your primary interest lies with federal laws, since these are the ones which sometimes offer difficulties in the way of obedience.

As an example of laws which are difficult to obey, one would first pick out the antitrust laws as the most striking. Without going into details in the matter, the experience of business for a generation or more has been that government policy and the interpretation of the laws on which that policy is based are not simple, direct, or clear. It is, for instance, difficult to tell whether enforcement is directed against monopoly or against bigness as such. There has been to my knowledge no occasion in which any administration has outlined its enforcement policy. In consequence, that enforcement has appeared arbitrary and unpredictable.

Without having followed the Federal and Supreme Courts' decisions in detail, it would appear that bigness has been established as a criterion for monopoly. At the same time, it appears that there is no court-established scale of bigness which may be depended upon as a guide in predicting administrative action under the laws. This makes it very difficult for the larger business firms to be sure they are keeping the law as administered and thus are carrying out their responsibilities toward the government.

The public has a definite interest in this question in those cases where low prices result from good business management applied to corporations of great size. There is in the public mind a sympathetic interest in support of small business; yet this sympathetic support seldom goes far enough to lead consumers to pay higher prices for goods because they are made or distributed by small firms instead of by great corporations.

In the distributing field particularly, the smaller store has to make its appeal in general on the basis of service, quality, and convenience. This, the consumer appreciates. It is doubtful if he would appreciate cracking down on the chain food stores or the great associations of department stores where these institutions are providing better goods at lower prices. To put it in fewer words: The best protection to bigness is efficiency, service, and low prices. That brings to them a measure of public support.

In this twilight zone, is it the duty of business to obey the law? This is hard to do in view of the fact that there is no definitive interpretation of the law by successive federal administrations.

Relations of business to government can best be analyzed if we think of these responsibilities as being to the people of the country as a whole. After all, the government represents its citizens as a whole, so that the duty of seeing to it that business does not act contrary to the interest of its citizens is one which government must assume in many cases. These cases thus represent a responsibility of business to government, though they do not come into play as active relationships between the two groups, unless and until business has failed in some important respect to observe the national interest.

Some of these cases, it is true, do lie definitely within the area of federal administration. As an example of this, the reciprocal trade treaties may be mentioned, particularly since the continuance of negotiations for such treaties is now up for decision before both houses of Congress.

It is in the interest of the people as a whole that there should be a larger volume of world trade and that the expansion of our own industries should be in the direction of products which we are most fit to produce, so that we may exchange them for other products which we are less fit to produce. Yet this general principle must not be carried to the point where existing industries are depressed. It simply means that future developments should be in the direction where a man-hour of American labor will bring to the consumer the highest worth, whether in domestically produced goods directly consumed, or exchanged in world markets for even higher values of foreign-produced goods.

The expansion of our import trade has other advantages besides that of raising the American standard of living. If any considerable part of the funds appropriated to ECA are to be repaid as loans rather than accepted as outright gifts, they will have to be repaid in large measure through imports from foreign countries or by our acceptance of services from them. We cannot get the money back as such, particularly in view of the fact that in general the money will not be exported as money but as goods.

Our ability to receive these imports and these services without damage to American industry is based upon the reasonable expectation that for the years immediately ahead we will have full employment and high production. It is unfortunate that employment and production will be based increasingly on our defense preparations. This makes it all the more necessary that we should be willing to receive scarce materials and desirable consumer goods which we ourselves are unable to furnish. We will thus simultaneously get some value for the billions spent abroad and in so doing increase our own consumption beyond what would be possible without this expansion of world trade.

In considering these general principles, we must not lose sight of the particular industries which are concerned. No industry has given me more concern in connection with these reciprocal trade treaties than has the woolen and worsted industry which forms such an important part of the employment and production of our whole New England area. To date, the figures are reassuring. Under the recent Geneva agreement, woolens and worsteds whose wool content was dutiable at forty and fifty cents per pound have had that duty reduced 25 per cent. The ad valorem duty of 35 or 45 per cent which was protective of domestic woolens has been reduced to 25 per cent; but this is subject to the right of the United States to increase this rate to 45 per cent ad valorem on imports of woolens and worsteds in any year wherein imports exceed 5 per cent of the average domestic production in the preceding three years. Since 1930 imports have never supplied more than 2 per cent of the domestic market. They consist chiefly of high quality fabrics that sell in the United States at higher prices than the bulk of domestic production.

The Labor Government estimates that the production in yards per man-hour in Great Britain is only half of that in the United States. It would seem that our more efficient operation and the very small total percentage of imports allowed without raising tariffs warrant our allowance of this small encouragement to British export and the corresponding effect in balancing the ERP payments which we are making to that country.

Perhaps I have spent too much time on this one question, but it seems to me that this is typical of the cases in which business has the duty of thinking nationally, and of refraining from active opposition so long as the injury is prospective rather than actual. This duty is made all the easier by the fact that any possible harm which may result to domestic interests is confined by the terms of the agreement to a very small percentage indeed, and it is doubtful whether real harm will result in the foreseeable future.

There is another group of problems with which we should be particularly concerned. That is the group which the general public assigns to government as its responsibility, but which the government is helpless to solve without the active assistance of business and other elements in the whole body of citizens. Perhaps the control of inflation is the best example.

It is generally assumed that the evils of inflation can be cured by government action. It is true that the federal government must play its part. It is true that as expenditures are cut down below income and the surplus is applied to the reduction of bank-held debt, such action tends to reduce inflationary pressure, though its effects may not be so direct as most people imagine. The best results come from holding the surplus in the Treasury.

But it is the regular experience of members of the Congress that every government expenditure has its proponents, many of whom are to be found in the ranks of business. As businessmen, we desire a particular expenditure, but would like to have expenditures in which other groups are interested denied to them or greatly curtailed. In this respect the businessman is no different from the farmer, or the wage earner, or the educator, or the representatives of other groups. We must remember that each one of them is as convinced of the rightfulness and desirability of his own project as are any of the rest.

Now the government can end inflation. Besides the fiscal and monetary policies and the helpful effect of a surplus, there are other and more drastic ways which really can end an inflation. Action can be taken through the Federal Reserve Board and the Treasury which will so tighten credit as to put brakes on business expansion. The brakes can be put on so hard that they will bring about business contraction. Business contraction can and will result in deflation.

The trouble with having government end inflation in this way is that it is an uncontrollable remedy. Nobody knows how big the dose should be. The reaction to any new dose may be moderate and beneficial; it may be immediate and drastic. The medicine may have a cumulative effect, so that after several applications without result, the whole then may take effect at once with catastrophic results. The uncertainties result from the fact that in these matters we are dealing with mass psychology rather than mass mechanics. Waves of hope and waves of fear in the business, investment, and speculative worlds cannot be measured or surely predicted. This makes it a dangerous process for the government to apply really drastic measures to end inflation.

There is another and very serious problem we have to face in trying to control the price level. It would be easier and safer to do it by any means whatever, were we not in a period of full employment and production. When we say "full employment," we do not mean that there is no one unemployed. We mean that of the two million or so not working, the larger part of them are out of work voluntarily, or at least temporarily. When we say "full production," we mean full production for a forty-hour week with the presently available production equipment, managerial ability, and assiduousness of the wage earner.

Such full employment and full production set the stage for our familiar spiral of increasing wages, costs, profits, and prices. The consumer prices again energize the new turn of the spiral and so on without any logical stopping point.

It is the most natural thing in the world for the wage earner to be confident of getting increased wages if the cost of living is increasing and if he knows he can get work elsewhere should his present employer not grant his requests. It is equally natural for the manufacturer or merchant to raise prices and increase profits if current wages are high enough to move their goods and services off the market as produced. Public purchasing power certainly will be sufficient to do so if the wage requests are granted.

All of this is natural, but may we not have to do something unnatural? The government is relatively helpless to act. Its endeavors to cut down expenditures meet added difficulty in the present and prospective yearly increases in our defense expenditures. These tend not only to add to the deficits and outstanding bank credit and purchasing power, but at the same time withdraw men from the active production of consumer goods and services.

More money for less goods is the formula for increased inflation. As we have seen, it is dangerous for the government to apply the more drastic remedies of credit contraction. Is there really anything else to fall back on except the development of new statesmanship on the part of business and organized labor? Is not the development of this statesmanship a duty which they owe to government, and particularly to government as the representative in this field of the general body of its citizens?

One point where labor statesmanship needs developing is in connection with the encouragement of the flow of profits into new labor-saving equipment. This raises the production per man-hour. This is the way in which the standard of living has been raised in the generations past. It is a main dependence of our hope for the future. The wage earner has a heavy stake in the accumulation and investment of profits.

The requirement for statesmanship is very necessary in employer-employee relations in such industries as coal, steel, oil, automobiles, and the great equipment industries, particularly those making durable consumer goods.

Fortunately, there have been evidences of late that this sense of public responsibility has been growing. Some months ago the Ford Motor Company and the International Harvester Company experimentally reduced their prices. Increased labor costs and lack of support by other elements in the industries compelled these firms to abandon the undertaking. Later on, in the important field of building materials, the largest lumber company in the world, the Weyerhaeuser Timber Company, made a similar experiment in price reduction. Its largest competitors looked on with interest, but without taking action. Not being willing to support the movement alone, the Weyerhaeuser Company withdrew its lower prices. Following this, General Electric reduced prices of durable consumer goods. The United States Steel Corporation, after a period of raising prices on certain of its products, later announced reductions on materials which entered particularly into the production of consumer goods. Westinghouse also announced certain reductions.

On the labor front, the United Automobile Workers negotiated with General Motors a settlement which can properly be termed statesmanlike. There is evidence that it is having its effect on other critical negotiations, which it was feared would lead to another serious round of the inflationary spiral. Business and labor statesmanship seems to be catching on. John L. Lewis has yet to be heard from.

All of this is in many respects foreign to the free enterprise system as we have known it. If the free enterprise system is to survive this crisis of the inflationary influence of high employment and production, it must adjust itself to this new procedure. For as yet there is no alternative except drastic governmental controls, and those spell out the end of free private enterprise.

What is required is an evolution of our system, instead of its destruction. Our system is based on the faith announced by Adam Smith that, in the sum total, selfish interests work together for the general good. The time has come when that doctrine is no longer tenable in its historic form.

If, however, we learn to distinguish between shortsighted selfish interests and long-range selfish interests, then the whole formula still applies and still will work with this simple readjustment of one of its elements.

We may still be selfish, but let us be selfish in the long-range view. What harm will there be if the disinterested observer finds it difficult to distinguish our selfishness from old-fashioned virtue?

THE RESPONSIBILITIES OF THE BUSINESSMAN TO THE CONSUMER

BY

Jack I. Straus

PRESIDENT
R. H. MACY AND CO., INC.
NEW YORK, NEW YORK

No other type of business gets as close to the consumer as retailing. Finance is several places removed, and so is most manufacturing. But the retailer is on the front line, observing consumer wants, checking on consumer reactions, making continuous judgments, and reaching basic conclusions about the relations between business and consumers. And when that retailer has grown to be the world's largest store, as Macy's has, you can be sure that an extraordinary job has been done of living up to responsibilities to consumers. But it's just as important, in the long run, for manufacturing and finance to heed those same responsibilities; the only difference between them and the retailer is that it takes a bit longer for the impact to reach them . . . Jack I. Straus, president of R. H. Macy and Company, gives us first-hand information about that impact. Like the other contributors, he has taken an active interest in business and civic activities; and like Mr. Deupree, he is a member of the Harvard Business School Visiting Committee. He is a director of some ten companies, including the Mutual Broadcasting System, L. Bamberger and Company of Newark, New Jersey, and Davison Paxon Company of Atlanta, Georgia.

THE RESPONSIBILITIES OF THE BUSINESSMAN TO THE CONSUMER

It is appropriate that a conference having as its subject "The Responsibilities of Business Leadership," should be held under the auspices of the Harvard Business School. We are dealing here with a problem of education — education of business and by business. The need for education does not end with a college degree. Sometimes I think it only begins there.

Certainly today the need for constant re-education grows, as conditions — world conditions, living conditions, business conditions, labor conditions — change so swiftly. We do not live in a static world, nor do we operate in a static business atmosphere. The conditions under which we live and work are volatile and dynamic, and we must remain alert to the requirements of changing methods to meet changing situations. Now, to a greater degree than ever before, we must keep abreast of developments. We must keep continuously informed as to what is going on, and what people are thinking.

My assignment is to discuss the consumer and the responsibilities of business to her. (I shall be referring to the customer as "her" or "she" because in the department store business "she" is responsible for 85 per cent of all purchases; and there is a strong suspicion that she exerts more than a casual influence on the other 15 per cent.) Most of what I say will reflect the retailer's point of view, but I believe that much of it is applicable to all business.

On most subjects in business you can get an argument. At least, that is true in the department store business. One economist says that sales in the next quarter will be good. Another says they will be bad. One merchant says inventories should be larger. Another says they should be smaller. How much should we spend for advertising? If I say "less," my associates rise up in wrath and say "more." Should our sales force be expanded? Some say "yes," others say "no." Every question, except one, invites difference of opinion, debate, disagreement.

What is this one, the one topic upon which all businessmen are in agreement, where you will get no debate? It is this: that the consumer is all-important. Her interests come before anything else. Everything you do, everything you sell, your profits, your future, depend upon her good will.

This is so obvious a truism that you may wonder why I lead off with it. If the customer, her interests, and her satisfactions, actually are so all-important, and if businessmen are in such unanimous agreement on the point, it would seem to be axiomatic then that all business would be conducted on a basis that would protect the customer's interests and insure her satisfaction at all times. Is this the case? No, too often it is not.

Take retailing as one example out of the many that could be cited. I imagine we would all agree that certain things were fairly fundamental to the satisfactory conduct of a retail store. The customer, if she is so important, would seem to be entitled to these things: She should be able to find the article she came in to buy, at the price she wanted to pay for it. She should be able to select it in an atmosphere that makes her visit a pleasant experience. She should be able to shop in surroundings that are clean and well kept. The person who waits on her and who takes her money should be courteous, helpful, and intelligent; he should know the merchandise he is selling and be equipped to describe its quality accurately and honestly; he should be able to instruct the customer as to how to take care of it to get the most enjoyment from it. She is also entitled to be thanked for having spent her money in your store instead of some other store. If the article turns out not to be satisfactory, or not as described, she is entitled to her money back, without question or argument.

She should be entitled to buy from the store's advertisement with perfect assurance that the advertisement is honest, factual, and complete. She is entitled not to be misled by the store's printed word any more than by the salesclerk's spoken word.

I think we would agree that all of this seems reasonable — and fundamental. Yet it is surprising how often this customer, this all-important element in the success of a business, fails to receive all the things she is entitled to. All too often the customer will visit a store, looking forward with some expectancy to a pleasant shopping experience, and: (1) Be unable to find what she wants; or (2) be forced to pay more for it than she wants to pay; or (3) be treated indifferently, if not discourteously, by a salesclerk who is not adequately informed about the merchandise, and is personally unconcerned as to whether she makes a satisfactory sale or not; who is not trained to give proper instructions as to the use or care of the article; and who too often does not bother even to thank the customer for her patronage.

An article sold thus badly, perhaps even misrepresented as to its ability to withstand washing, ironing, and the like, may well not be satisfactory. And the customer, justifiably indignant, returns the article and too frequently is promptly enveloped in a welter of red tape. Obstacles arise which prevent or delay a satisfactory adjustment. Or she wants her money back, and sometimes she doesn't get it. And what started out to be a pleasant shopping experience has deteriorated into a vexing and disappointing episode from which all opportunity for good will has vanished.

So here is our paradox. Everyone agrees that the customer's interests and satisfactions are paramount, that the future of a business, any business, depends upon her good will — yet day after day in all kinds of contacts with that customer, business fails to do everything that is required to protect her interests and, still more serious, permits her confidence to be undermined.

Perhaps you think I have overstated the case. Most businesses are reasonably well run. Take Macy's as an example. Macy's has long had a reputation of being an efficiently run store. Out of every 10,000 transactions we get only 75 recorded complaints. That might seem to indicate that 9,925 out of every 10,000 are satisfied customers. But that is nothing to be complacent about. We must be acutely sensitive to those 75. They represent only the 75 we heard from, those who took the trouble to complain. What about those who weren't satisfied but didn't bother to tell us about it?

So long as the customer has the right of free choice and the right to say "No! I will do my business somewhere else," she has the ultimate success or failure of any business in her hands. Those 75 aren't 75 at all — they are 75 multiplied by all the people to whom they talk. Unless we are sensitive and vigilant the 75 can become a hundred and the hundred a thousand. That is where good will disappears and businesses, in time, disappear with it.

No — there is no room for complacency, we must do more about our obligations to our customers than talk about them. It is time that all of us had a very careful look at ourselves, made an objective and painstaking inventory of our customer relations, and a meticulous correction of our failures to meet our specific obligations to the customers who keep us in business.

If some of the things I have mentioned, and will mention further, seem elementary it is because we are dealing here with an elementary set of problems that must be met by specific and "grass roots" means.

I have the feeling that nowadays too many businessmen are so preoccupied with the more abstract problems which confront them that they either overlook or take for granted the fundamentals.

In my own business the fundamentals are at the point of sale. It is not possible for us to remain long unaware of customer dissatisfaction. Yet we are guilty, too, of daily derelictions of the kind I have been describing earlier. How is it possible for a business to have sound policies yet be guilty of unsatisfactory execution of those policies? How can we be assured that the resolves of top management will be carried down the line properly? That indifferent salesclerk I mentioned a moment ago, is she to blame for having been guilty of bad customer contact? No, the blame must rest with those who administer the business, that their policies are not being intelligently taught and interpreted. And the underlying seriousness of this, of course, is that primary obligations to the customer are being neglected.

Now a word about these primary or immediate obligations to the customer, and some with longer-range implications. In the case of the retail business these primary or immediate responsibilities are: to have the merchandise the customer wants, at the price she wants to pay; to display it attractively and make it easy for her to make her selection; to advertise it truthfully; to sell it intelligently and courteously; to stand back of any article sold; to make adjustments promptly and fairly; and to surround every transaction with whatever service facilities the customer requires.

Now let us consider a few longer-range responsibilities.

First, the question of price. When a retailer places his price on an article he makes the final claim on the consumer's dollar for all the costs and profits of the factors of production and distribution. The farmer and worker, manager and investor, bondholder and tax collector — all must be covered in the retailer's delivered price. It is the retailer's responsibility to the community to make sure that the value of the merchandise when it reaches the consumer is as great as possible, or, to put it another way, to make sure the merchandise is made available for final use at the lowest possible price.

I have said many times before, and I must say again, we must fight for a lower level of prices on which depends the maintenance of a standard of living adequate to support a prosperous United States. Price fixing and price maintenance are devices aimed at keeping prices up and as such are dangerous to the community and inimical to the interests of the consumer. She loses the effect of competition at the retail level and cannot benefit from the search for lower price lines that is characteristic of retail competition. When a manufacturer fixes or maintains a price, the price must be high enough to satisfy the high-cost distributor, and the community is deprived of the economies of mass distribution at retail and the lower prices that would inevitably result.

Second, the matter of quality. Here, as in so many things, we find it necessary to protect the customer from the store. Does that strike you as a curious thing for me to say? Here is what I mean by it. So imperfectly is our dependence upon the customer understood that when a person goes to work for us he appears to believe that he is now working for the store as against the customer. I had occasion to ask this question of our Training Squad some time ago, "Do you believe that it is your job to protect the store against the customer, or the customer against the store?" You must realize that our Training Squad is made up of young men and women, new to the business, many of them just out of college. They are beginning their business careers. Now let me repeat my question: "Do you believe that it is your job to protect the store against the customer, or the customer against the store?" Ninety-nine per cent of them said, "To protect the store against the customer." You can see why I keep repeating that our job is one of constant education on fundamentals, and that it is fatal to take them for granted.

Stores are made up of people — young, energetic, enthusiastic people, working at a very fast pace. Buyers with highly developed technical skills constantly scouting markets, here and abroad, for new, different, interesting things. Advertising people, also young, energetic, enthusiastic, constantly devising novel and ingenious ways of selling merchandise. Merchandisers, stylists, management people — all geared to the rapid tempo of today's retail operation.

Before any buyer is allowed to advertise his merchandise to the public, before an advertising writer is allowed to write final copy for an ad, the protective elements are put to work. The buyer must submit his merchandise to the Macy Bureau of Standards to be tested, and the advertising writer must submit his copy to the Bureau of Standards to be approved for accuracy. This Bureau of Standards was set up in Macy's over twenty years ago to protect the customer against the human failings of buyers and advertising writers. It is our watchdog of quality and accuracy. It reports to the president. Its word is law.

Sometimes a manufacturer makes unjustified claims as to the quality of his product, or of the fabric content, or as to the way it will perform in use. Before we offer it to the public, the Bureau of Standards must test those claims, and approve them. We must do this if we are in earnest about our obligations to the customer.

We carry over 400,000 different articles, bought from more than 15,000 manufacturers. Not all of them have the facilities or the desire to produce only articles of good quality. Some of them don't know how and some of them don't care. But we have to care. That merchandise is going to be sold in our store, to our customers. It is basically our good will that is at stake.

The Bureau of Standards in Macy's has another function, and that brings me to my third long-range responsibility of the retailer to his customer: the requirement to improve existing products and develop new and better ones.

Let me give you a recent example. Macy's sells a

wide variety of play clothes for children. Not long ago the head of our Bureau of Standards read where a boy had been fatally burned because the cowboy suit he was wearing had caught fire. He went to the department where cowboy suits are sold and asked for a sample of every type of playsuit we carry. These he tested, and found that many were highly inflammable. He returned to the department and ordered every playsuit taken off sale. Then he contacted the manufacturers involved, solicited and got their interest in correcting this problem, put them in touch with a firm which had developed a fireproofing substance, and today Macy's sells only playsuits which our tests have shown to be safe from this particular hazard. And, of course, we have gone to manufacturers in other lines of children's apparel to duplicate this process. Thus, out of a retailer's long-range interest in the customer's welfare (in this case, safety), the customer is better off, the store is better off, and the manufacturer is better off.

My last example of the long-range obligation of the retailer to the customer is, in a sense, to protect the customer against herself. Here I refer to the elusive subject of taste. It used to be popular among stores to carry at least 25 per cent of their merchandise in bad taste because "that was what people wanted." Forward-looking merchants realized that to sell a customer an article in bad taste was as serious a dereliction as selling her something of bad quality. Realizing that their customers were of uneven educational backgrounds, stores tacitly rather than obviously began a process of educating the tastes of their customers. I don't mean that to sound patronizing, but it is what happened. And when I say educate their customers, I also mean educating their buyers and manufacturers as well.

I remember twenty-five years ago when Macy's began to grow conscious of its responsibility in this connection. We hired stylists, whose job it was to eliminate from our stocks the monstrosities and to substitute for them things of good taste. The stylist working with the buyer was charged with the same responsibility for taste that the buyer had for quality and price. In those days, there was serious conflict between the two, for the buyer naturally favored carrying anything that had a ready sale, while the stylist was critical of the style value. Since then this problem has been resolved with the buyer accepting the overall dictate of the stylist on "looks-rightness," but it represented a great deal of work and a great deal of education — of ourselves, of manufacturers, and of our customers. It was another element added to the process of raising the American standard of living.

The mail-order houses in time did the same thing. Compare the Sears, Roebuck catalogue today with that of fifteen or twenty years ago. And, by the way, compare Sears, Roebuck's sales today with those of fifteen or twenty years ago.

People in this country want better things, better-made things and better-looking things, and they want to pay less for them, so they may enjoy more of them. That, reduced to simple terms, is the American way of life. We must remember the significance in this country of a Ford automobile selling for around five hundred dollars. We must remember the significance of F. W. Woolworth's five and ten cent store concept. More things for more people, selling in vast quantities at relatively low prices, providing millions of jobs to people who make and sell them. But do we understand that the key to the whole equation is low prices and greater aggregate profits produced by lesser unit profits spread over more articles made and sold? Sometimes I wonder whether either business or labor understands the nature of the American goose and its golden eggs.

Earlier, I said that business needed to do more about its responsibilities to the consumer than merely talk about them. I would like to conclude with six suggestions of things we might do.

1. Set out to know the customer again. Find out all you can about her through a continuous program of objective customer research. Find out what she wants to buy; find out what she wants to pay for it; ask her what she thinks of your product or your store or your service.

2. Restudy your business on the basis of what your customer tells you she thinks of you and wants from you. Remember — you are in business to please her.

3. Take an inventory of the devices you have or should have to protect your customer against human failings in your business. If you don't protect her against your shortcomings, she will protect herself against them.

4. Review the policies that determine the accuracy, honesty, and usefulness to the customer of your advertising. Many surveys have established that the customer wants more facts in advertising. Are you giving them to her?

5. Consider what are your responsibilities in the field of consumer education. What are you doing to help the customer understand and know your business, your product, your store? She wants to know more about you. All consumer studies have indicated that very plainly. Why not develop a program so that you tell her, rather than leave it to some consumer group which may be on your side or may not?

6. Take a look at the long-range obligations you have to the customer in the matter of price, quality, good taste, safety, and the like. What steps can you take to develop a better article at a lower price, in better style, safer to use?

These are a few of the responsibilities towards that all-important person — the consumer. In these fundamentals lie the elements that separate greatness from mediocrity. History already records the progress of those business statesmen who through their able leadership have created great institutions out of small beginnings. Certainly, the reward is impressive for both the businessman and his customer.

MANAGEMENT'S RESPONSIBILITIES TO STOCKHOLDERS

BY

Harry A. Bullis

CHAIRMAN OF THE BOARD
GENERAL MILLS, INC.
MINNEAPOLIS, MINNESOTA

It has been said that the stockholder is the real forgotten man. He has certainly made fewer gains in the past fifteen years than, for example, the worker; though considerable argument rages as to whether that is good or bad. But one question is beyond dispute: The businessman has definite responsibilities to the stockholder, which must be met just as his responsibilities to other groups must be met . . . Harry A. Bullis, chairman of the board of General Mills, is particularly qualified to discuss these responsibilities, for two reasons: first, because his company has done an excellent job of living up to them; and, second, because it has tried new and important methods in developing closer relations with stockholders . . . Most of Mr. Bullis' career has been with General Mills and its predecessor companies. He became secretary and controller of General Mills when it was organized in 1928, and he moved up steadily until, last year, he was named chairman of the board of directors. He is a trustee of the National Planning Association and of the Committee for Economic Development; and a director of the United States Chamber of Commerce and of the Northwest Bancorporation.

MANAGEMENT'S RESPONSIBILITIES TO STOCKHOLDERS

During the early years of this century, expansion and production, almost exclusively, occupied the country's best business minds. The years between the two world wars were characterized by tremendous emphasis on selling and merchandising. I hope and believe that the second half of our century will be marked by inspiring progress in the field of human relations. I am confident that, through determined effort and the exercise of tolerance and human understanding, the many intricate group relationships of our modern world can and will be harmonized.

The developments of our postwar economy have brought into sharp focus the interdependence of the four major groups in our free competitive system: management, labor, stockholder, and consumer. More and more the leaders of these groups are coming to realize the need for sound thinking and sincere co-operation if all are to enjoy to the full the benefits of our way of life. We are gradually learning that each group has duties and responsibilities as well as rights, and that we all stand to gain more through coöperation than through controversy. It is indicative of the trend of American thought that a meeting should be devoted to a discussion of the social responsibilities of business.

Under our freely competitive economy — our "people's capitalism" as Harold Stassen calls it — management acts as a balance wheel for the interests of employees, stockholders, and the consuming public. It is in a position of trusteeship for each of these groups. Management has the duty of seeing that no one group gains unreasonable advantage at the expense of the others.

If sound management can maintain the proper balance, all groups prosper. But if one group gains an unreasonable advantage at the expense of the others, there is danger of business failure and consequent hardship to all.

These interrelationships have been greatly complicated by the tremendous growth of American industry. Seventy-five or a hundred years ago, the average business was small, and it was usually owned by one man or by a partnership of two or three. The office was probably a corner of the shop or mill. The business was managed by the owner, and he knew personally the men who worked for him — knew their faults, their special abilities, and the members of their families. Thus the proprietor combined in his own person the functions of management and ownership, and he was closely identified with labor also. Such were the conditions which existed in the year 1866 when Governor C. C. Washburn built his first flour mill in Minneapolis on the Falls of St. Anthony.

Today, we who manage the company which evolved from Governor Washburn's early initiative face a very different situation. The company — General

Mills — is owned by over 12,000 shareholders living in every state of the union, and it has 12,500 employees. Management has emerged as an entity separate from ownership and labor, yet its obligations to both, and to the public, are more important than ever.

I shall discuss one of these responsibilities of management — that of stockholder relations.

First of all, what does the progressive and independent stockholder want and expect of management?

"Above all he wants to be treated as an owner and a partner in the enterprise and not merely as a name on a stock ledger." So says Mr. Lewis Gilbert of New York, unquestionably the country's most ardent campaigner for the rights of small stockholders. That is how the stockholder *ought* to feel. It is how progressive management *wants* him to feel. But unfortunately, in a great many cases, stockholders are apathetic. They stay away from annual meetings in droves. Few ever visit their companies or write letters to the officers. It becomes, therefore, the responsibility of management to stimulate this interest on the part of its stockholders, to try to awaken them to the responsibilities of ownership.

We believe that the way to arouse the interest of stockholders is by friendly personal contact. Much can be accomplished by annual reports, dividend inserts, and stockholder magazines, but printed matter can never take the place of personal contact. Any publication is, at best, a one-way avenue, and the essence of sound relations between owner and manager is frank and unimpeded two-way communication.

This was the reasoning that led our founder and former board chairman, James F. Bell, in 1938 to pioneer informal regional meetings with stockholders throughout the country. At these gatherings we meet personally about 25 per cent of our owners. These meetings were discontinued during the war, but were resumed in the autumn of 1946. The practice of holding such informal meetings is being followed by a growing number of companies interested in improving stockholder relations. The informal meeting offers wide possibilities. It gives owners and managers the opportunity to become acquainted and to learn from each other, and results in the establishment of confidence and mutual respect.

It has been the custom for the chairman to greet each stockholder personally at the door as he or she arrives for the meeting. We have avoided the use of a stage or platform of any kind, in order to be free to move among the audience in a friendly and informal manner. This has been particularly effective during the period of questions-and-answers with which we conclude each meeting.

With this approach it has been possible, in a tactful way, to emphasize the stockholder's responsibility to management — the need, as Mr. Bell puts it, for each owner to "get behind the company morally and spiritually as well as financially." We have therefore made the personal approach the keystone of our whole stockholder relations program. Our purpose is to establish the *we* relationship. When an owner writes to me and suggests that *we* — rather than *you* or *they* — should do this or that, then I know that we have been making real progress in our stockholders' program.

Our personal relations with a new stockholder commence the moment we receive his name on the purchase records. They do not end until he has sold his stock, and even then reluctantly and with the hope of future reunion.

Initial contact with a stockholder is a personal letter addressed to him by the president of the company welcoming him into "the General Mills family." This letter also offers the new stockholder, as a gift, a box of our assorted grocery products, to be mailed to him or to whomever he designates. A follow-up letter goes to each stockholder who requests the gift box. A special letter from the president also goes to every employee who becomes a stockholder, making the same offer of free products. These "welcome" letters start off the owner-management relationship in a friendly way. Our files are full of appreciative letters from owners who are surprised and delighted at this personal interest. Another letter is sent to the stockholder if he sells his stock. This is also from the president, and expresses the hope that no action on the part of management has caused the stockholder to decide to sell and that he will soon again be numbered among the company's owners. Each stockholder who mails in his proxy for the annual meeting receives a letter of thanks from the president.

An important though secondary benefit which we hope to derive from stockholder coöperation is the word-of-mouth salesmanship which owners can give to company products. We found that, in spite of a fairly active stockholder program and a very low rate of stock turnover, only a little over half of our stockholders were able to identify the company's nationally advertised products; still fewer used them in their own homes or recommended them to friends. In an attempt to familiarize owners with the products of the company, and make them active users and boosters of these products, we inaugurated a Christmas gift package and made it available at cost to all stockholders and employees for mailing to their friends. Several thousand of these boxes were shipped in the Christmas season of 1947.

Likewise, whenever we introduce a new product, we send a complimentary package to every owner who indicates a desire to receive it by mailing a return post card inserted in our stockholders' publication. When Apple Pyequick was placed on the market in the fall of 1946, 50 per cent of the owners requested packages.

Enclosures sent with dividend checks can also be used effectively to familiarize owners with company products. Recently we printed a stockholders' memo pad which is a case in point. As a reminder, it shows our major products in four colors. It is attention-getting, and we hope it will do a good job when it is mailed out with the next dividend check.

Another dividend insert, which is labeled "Read

About Yourself in the National Magazines," was mailed to General Mills stockholders with their dividend checks in May 1948. This one has a dual purpose. It once again calls attention to our consumer products, and it is also calculated to stimulate the reading of a national institutional advertisement which is reproduced on the inside page of the folder. This particular ad ran in four colors in the *Saturday Evening Post, Life, This Week,* the *American Weekly,* and several farm magazines, and attempted to answer the question, "Who owns General Mills?" Because of its subject matter, we believed it would be of particular interest to stockholders, and if they could be influenced to talk about it, so helping to spread the truth about company ownership, we would have made a small contribution toward clearing up a dangerous misconception currently existing in the public mind.

In 1947 Dr. Henry C. Link and the Psychological Corporation made a scientific study for the Controllership Foundation based on interviews with a thousand persons in twenty-eight cities from coast to coast. These one thousand persons were a cross section of the nation's adult urban population. The study revealed that almost one-third of the people agree with the statement that "a handful of men like the DuPonts, Rockefellers, and Fords own most of the corporations in America." Eight out of ten admit they have no idea as to the number of persons who own a big corporation. One person in five guesses that big corporations are usually owned by fewer that one hundred people.

Most people simply do not realize that the owners of big corporations are the general public — ordinary people who have spare money to invest; that more women than men own stock; and that owners are widely scattered throughout the country, not centered in Wall Street and the East.

In this advertisement we tried to dramatize a typical stockholder situation — a widow and her high-school son. In simple dialogue form, the boy's mother points out that General Mills' stock is broadly held by many small stockholders throughout the country, that women stockholders predominate, and that last year our employees' "take" was over six times that of the stockholders. It would be folly to imagine that this one ad, despite its exposure to some twenty-seven million readers, will correct the erroneous ideas which so many people have about the ownership of corporations as revealed in Dr. Link's survey. But it will help. And if other companies will also present the facts with respect to their ownership, these combined efforts will have a noticeably positive effect.

The annual report is the most important document prepared for stockholders. We are all aware of the evolution that has taken place in annual reports during the past decade. Our General Mills reports have undergone the transition from dry, conventional, strictly financial statements to what we hope are interesting, readable summaries of the year's work. In addition to the necessary financial data, they now touch on the philosophy of management, and discuss the major problems we face and the current situation with respect to such matters as labor relations, research and the development of new products, plant expansion, advertising, and public service. Pictures, drawings, and charts help liven the pages, and an effort is made to avoid columns of small print and statistics.

Because of the character of our business — necessitating as it does tremendous purchases of wheat throughout the harvest season — it is not feasible to issue interim or quarterly financial statements, because they would reflect a badly distorted fiscal picture. Instead we publish, in addition to the Annual Report, two small quarterly magazines for stockholders: *Progress Thru Research,* which keeps owners up to date on the technical developments of our research laboratories, and *General Mills Horizons,* which attempts to cover the whole field of stockholder interests. Before *Horizons* was introduced in 1947, we mailed a questionnaire to stockholders in order to learn what type of subject matter would be most interesting to them. A surprisingly large number of responses — over 2500 — were received and they revealed that the subjects in which a good percentage of our owners are interested are: first, new products, new facilities, research, and plans for the future; second, profits and financial outlook; third, current problems facing the company; fourth, policies of the company and the reasons behind them; fifth, the company's products and services.

Some five hundred owners not only marked the questionnaire, but also took the trouble to give us some additional suggestions and comments. A good many praised the company's policy of keeping stockholders well informed through publications and informal meetings. Many asked for Betty Crocker recipes. This is a reflection of the growing number of women stockholders — 44 per cent of our owners are women. Quite a number suggested that stories on distribution, sales, advertising, human relations, home appliances, products control, and nutrition should be printed in *Horizons*.

Among the questionnaires returned were several that reflected a good sense of humor. I am reminded of one in particular. The questionnaire had several suggested subjects for the new stockholders' magazine. One was "Biographies of the men who built General Mills." After this statement the stockholder had written, "I have read a history of the company and most of the founders led such hard-working and God-fearing lives that their biographies would make very dull reading!" Accordingly, we have included no biographies of the founding fathers.

One of the major points made by Lewis Gilbert in his discussion of the rights of small stockholders is that they should receive a full report of what takes place at the formal annual stockholders' meeting. Surprising as it may seem, a number of corporations are still resisting the issuance of such post-meeting reports to their stockholders. The majority, however, have recognized this as one of the responsibilities of management to stockholders, and are putting out attractive, specially prepared reports. Standard Oil Company of New Jersey sends every stockholder a full stenographic report of the proceedings. We have followed the practice of including the minutes of the meetings in our stockholders' publication, *Horizons.* We also include pictures taken at the meeting, as well as other graphic material.

Even better, however, is a report given in person. This was the idea behind Mr. Bell's inauguration a decade ago of the informal stockholders' meeting. Our formal annual stockholders' meeting is held in Wilmington, Delaware, in August. Considering the midsummer heat and the not-too-convenient location, it is not remarkable that only a handful of owners attend it. At meetings held in the fall in convenient metropolitan centers, Mr. Bell has been able to summarize the year's work and also report to the owners on what happened at the formal annual meeting. He regards the chairman of the board as a "personal ambassador of the stockholders to management" whose duty it is not only to interpret management to the owners but also to be their active and direct representative in the affairs of the company which they own. To discharge this responsibility, the chairman must have personal contact with the stockholders.

Some owners come as far as two hundred miles to attend these informal gatherings in New York, Buffalo, Washington, Boston, Chicago, Detroit, Minneapolis, San Francisco, and Los Angeles. The meetings are held over a period of about a month's time. The atmosphere is kept informal and personal throughout, starting with a personal invitation from the chairman to attend. Displays of the company's products, activities, and services are on view in the meeting room, which is usually in one of the large hotels. Attendance runs between a hundred and fifty and five hundred people. After a brief talk by the chairman, a motion picture — especially produced for the occasion — is presented. This leads naturally into discussion, and is followed by a lively question-and-answer session. A social period, with coffee and cake and samplings of company products, brings the meeting to a close. The entire affair is well paced and lasts less than one hour and a half.

The motion picture films developed for these meetings are based on the Annual Report. They interpret the report in easily understood visual form. Later on, they become important tools in our public relations program with employees, business organizations, students, and other groups. Our 1946 movie, "Operation 46," was awarded the first "Oscar" to be given by *Financial World* magazine for an annual report film. We are currently at work on the film to be shown at our informal meetings next fall. As evidence of tangible results, I quote from *Exchange* magazine, the publication of the New York Stock Exchange:

> The personalized slant of General Mills published matter is evident; and this approach to the public and stockholders has long been followed. What results are in evidence?
>
> The common stock ended 1946 at 50¾, representing a rise of 2¼ points in a year marked by a sharp general relapse of share prices. The Dow Jones average for 30 industrial common stocks declined over 15½ points in 1946. At 50¾, General Mills common afforded a yield of 2.95%, against an average yield of 4.26% for stocks in

the Dow-Jones group. Obviously, the company's stockholders were content, during the market furore, to retain their holdings. A causal relationship existed between stockholder stability and the management's persistent program of enlightened stockholder relations.

I am convinced that if each industrial enterprise will take the trouble to explain its operations honestly and thoroughly — not only to stockholders but to employees and to the general public as well (making sure that those policies and operations are honest and ethical to begin with) — then business as a whole will be well along the way toward eliminating most of the unfair criticisms leveled against it.

A company that is "a good corporate citizen" — that produces a good product at a reasonable price; that pays its employees fairly; that rewards its owners with reasonable returns on their investment; that plans for the future with new and better products to raise the general living standard — such a company, if its story is told to the public, provides the best possible testimony for a free economy.

But to accomplish anything of lasting value in human relations, the program must be continuous, long range, year-to-year in scope.

Dr. Samuel Johnson once said: "A man, Sir, should keep his friendships in constant repair." His admonition might have been addressed to business. Good will cannot be written on the books overnight. And it can never be written to stay there without subsequent entries. All ink tends to fade in the ledger of public opinion. We must make our entries every day.

RESPONSIBILITIES OF BUSINESSMEN TO THE WORLD

BY

Allen W. Dulles

PARTNER, SULLIVAN & CROMWELL

NEW YORK, NEW YORK

Allen W. Dulles covers an area of business responsibility which might justifiably be called the newest. In the long run, it may also be the most important. The fact that American businessmen have responsibilities to the world beyond our borders, may be a comparatively new idea to business management. But after the tremendous events of the past fifteen years, who can possibly doubt that it is true? . . . Mr. Dulles is one of the leaders who early recognized this truth, and who has been fighting for many years to establish it in the minds of others. He would be the first to agree that his task is by no means completed; but his missionary work has brought great results . . . As a lawyer and partner in Sullivan and Cromwell, Mr. Dulles knows the problems, policies, and methods of business. He knows the world, too. He was in the United States Diplomatic Service for ten years, and has been a United States delegate or adviser on many international conferences and missions. He was awarded three decorations for his work with the Office of Strategic Services in Europe during the war. In 1946–47, Mr. Dulles was legal consultant to the Herter Committee on Foreign Aid; and he is now president of the Council on Foreign Relations and a director of the Woodrow Wilson Foundation.

RESPONSIBILITIES OF BUSINESSMEN TO THE WORLD

Today the people of more than one-half of the world are expecting our material aid and are calling on us for assistance in solving their problems. They are telling us that they cannot recover or even retain their freedom and independence without our help. Unless we close our eyes to reality, it is hard to find any very convincing arguments that they are wrong about this.

The United States has not consciously aspired to any such dominant world position. It is therefore somewhat startling to be brought face to face with these realities. We are unquestionably the most powerful and the most influential nation in the world. This is not said in any boastful spirit. It is rather a reluctant admission of an uncomfortable fact. We would probably be far safer and less harried if there were in the world a half-dozen other countries of comparable stature; countries which could share these difficult tasks with us.

This power of ours, whether it came sought or unsought, brings with it responsibilities and these responsibilities are in direct ratio to our power position in the world. In the case of individuals, we freely recognize that power brings responsibility. It is equally true of a nation.

The course to be charted by the United States to meet its world responsibilities is primarily a function of government operating through its free constitutional processes and under the critical eye of public opinion. From the events of the past year we can assume, I believe, that our government recognizes the general nature of our responsibilities and has substantial popular support in meeting them. But this backing is as yet far from unanimous and our policy is far from crystallized, though there are significant signs of the direction in which we are moving.

First of all, there is the European Recovery Program initiated just about a year ago. A few months earlier we had the somewhat startling adventure into Greece and Turkey with implications which have not yet been fully grasped. Very recently Senator Vandenberg, with the unanimous support of the Senate Foreign Relations Committee, introduced a most significant resolution. It called for the strengthening of the United Nations and for the effective association of the United States with regional arrangements essential to our security, such, for example, as that among the American states and the agreement between Britain, France, and the Benelux countries. This resolution has been overwhelmingly adopted by the Senate.

We have come far in less than twenty years. We have now recognized that our peace and security are bound up with the vigorous defense of the principles on which a free society is based, and that this defense must begin not at our shores but wherever in the world these principles are seriously threatened and where the threatened people are prepared to rally to their defense.

It will require not only wisdom and sound popular education but the consistent and effective employment of the great resources of the United States to carry such a policy to a successful and peaceful conclusion. It cannot be done by pious declarations or by government fiat. It calls for a contribution by the people of this country in ways other than by paying high taxes.

What is the proper role of American business leadership in the face of the responsibilities our government is assuming in the foreign field? What part should American business play in aid of its government in building up a strong, free, and friendly world society — a society which will insure the survival of free men and of free enterprise?

I propose to consider these questions from the viewpoint of the representative capacity of the businessman, that is to say, in his capacity as the manager or custodian of business enterprise and not in his individual capacity as a citizen. In this latter capacity the businessman, of course, shares with others the duties of citizenship, often enhanced by the fact that his position of power may give him added individual responsibility.

The first duty of American business is to protect the economy of the United States and to keep our position sound at home. A serious depression here might easily spell the end of our ability or, if not of our ability, of our willingness, to be effective in the foreign field.

It is difficult for the American mind to follow the subtleties of Soviet policy, but there appears to be one clear note in it. The Russians are banking on an early depression in the United States to end effective action on our part abroad. This may partly explain their strange maneuvers with regard to the Marshall Plan.

Outwardly it would seem that they have played into the hands of the proponents of the European Recovery Program. Their bold frontal attack on the plan at Paris a year ago, followed up with open and public sabotage of every measure toward joint recovery by the European powers, rallied to the plan even the wavering in Western Europe and in the American Congress. This was followed by their cynical veto against participation by the economically hungry satellite states and the publicly organized Cominform to fight American aid to Europe. We, the warmongers, according to Vishinsky, are merely attempting to meet an "impending crisis" by "accelerated exports to Europe." If this fails, the Soviet leaders tell the world that we will resort to war to save capitalism.

Soviet observers in the United States can hardly have failed to tell the Kremlin that their course of action was solidifying American opinion in support of aid to European recovery. Yet they went right ahead with their tactics. If the Soviet had subtly simulated agreement, sought large grants in aid and then sabotaged from within, it is doubtful, to say the least, that the Marshall Plan would be in effect today.

Of course, it is not easy for the Soviets to alter overnight long-range ideological and propaganda policies. But had they not been confident that the recovery plan would fail, they might have tempered their attitude towards the ERP and not been reconciled to see us put it into effect.

The USSR has not forgotten that after World War I America had two depressions in a little over ten years during the period of adjusting our economy to postwar conditions. If these economic dislocations in the capitalist system took place after World War I, the Soviet expects that we will soon have even more serious economic disturbances, as the physical and moral destruction in World War II far exceeded that of the first war. They are gambling on the fact that the capitalist world, and the United States in particular, faces a depression exceeding in violence those of the 1920's and 1930's. If so, the Soviet expects the United States to pull out of Europe and Asia irrespective of commitments. Then, they argue, these great areas will fall into the communist lap, and our influence will be even less than if we had had no Marshall Plan. We shall have put our hand to the plow and turned back.

Here is a challenge to American business leadership. A serious recession in business during the next few years, before our war-exhausted friends and allies are back on their feet, might well turn into a world catastrophe. The Soviet system profits from chaos and failure. It is our task to build and construct. Ours is the harder role, and to meet its challenge we must remain strong here at home. This is the first responsibility of American business leadership to the world.

The second area of business responsibility lies in the

foreign field. What contribution can business make to promote recovery abroad?

There can be no political recovery in economic chaos. Hungry, idle people rarely exercise sane political judgments. The democratic, liberal forms of government which we consider necessary if man is to realize his true capabilities wither away under conditions of economic and social distress. It is then that men, fearful for their very survival, despairing of their own capacity to grapple with the complications of modern life, turn in desperation to leaders who exact even the surrender of body, soul, and property in return for a promised but fanciful security.

Hence, the future of the political system under which we live may well depend upon world economic revival. This, in turn, is impossible unless leadership comes from the United States. We alone have the tools and the resources. But we must share with a stricken world not only material things. We must also share our technical skills, manpower, and our organizational ability.

It is here that American business comes into the picture. It has something to contribute that a government alone cannot supply. If we stand on this side of the Atlantic and dole out food and goods and money alone, the Marshall Plan will fail and no plan like it would succeed. If, on the other hand, we turn the European Recovery Plan into a genuine coöperative effort supported by the business brains and ability of the United States, plus the resources we can put into the venture, we have a chance of success. For this, new sources of wealth must be tapped. New fields of enterprise must be explored in the African and American continents and elsewhere. We must again call on the type of farseeing business genius which our pioneers showed in developing the North American continent and which the founders of Britain's great empire evidenced in the eighteenth and nineteenth centuries.

Private American business enterprise, however, is not organized for the purpose of carrying out governmental policy or embarking on purely humanitarian or philanthropic ventures, either in the foreign field or in the domestic field, even though the objective may be both righteous and important. I am not speaking here, of course, of the legitimate contributions which, under law, business, as well as private individuals, can and should make to charitable enterprises, nor to the vast expenditure of private business in the field of research which inures to the public benefit as well as to private gain. The profit motive is and must remain the basic justification for business to engage in a particular enterprise, though profit need not be interpreted in the sense of immediate dollars and cents. Incidental or long-range benefit to business may be enough. But we cannot expect those who have the responsibility to manage the resources entrusted to American business to venture into the foreign field merely because to do so might aid American policy. The directors of American business are the trustees for the enterprises entrusted to them, not for the nation at large. If business starts to play the part of a "vicarious philanthropist" or becomes the handmaid of the policy maker, it will fail in its primary duty. It may even endanger the sound basis of domestic economy. Further than that, business in such a role would be crossing over the gap between the totalitarian state where business is merely a function of government and the free state where business stands on its own feet.

In this connection it is interesting to recall that in 1937 when the Nazi experiment was at its height, the German corporate law was amended to read substantially as follows: The management on its own responsibility must so conduct the company as to advance the welfare of the enterprise and of its personnel *and the general advantage of the state and of the people* (Gemeine nutzen von Volk und Reich). The concluding phrase of this law is seemingly quite innocuous. At first glance it appeals to our humanitarian and civic impulses. But provisions such as these became the weapons whereby the totalitarian state shackled free enterprise. The Nazis used this very law to get their hands on business.

The author of this high-sounding formula was none other than a notorious Nazi, Undersecretary in the Ministry of Justice and double-barrelled doctor, Dr. Dr. Franz Schlegelberger. In his commentary on this law, the doctor announced that this legislation introduced the "Führer" principle into the corporation law. Before this, he remarked, irresponsible stockholders exercised their rights for their own benefit. The new law, he said, has broken with this idea and management henceforth must act in the interest of the people and the state. The supreme laws governing management were to be National Socialist principles.

Business can best serve the state by adhering to the principle of its responsibilities to those whom it employs, to those whom it serves, and to those who own it. If business is also generally to serve the state and state policy under rules prescribed by the state, it will soon find that it has lost its birthright.

Business is regulated by law. Limitations are placed on its activities in the public interest through the antitrust legislation and a host of other laws. This is as it should be, but business should not be under vague mandates enforcible by the state. This is the way of totalitarianism.

However, business has a real and a legitimate stake in the success of governmental policy and, in particular, in the success of our foreign policy. This would mean broader markets for the products of American business. It would mean increased purchasing power and finally, but most important of all, it would mean that the system of free enterprise may gain a sufficiently broad basis in the world to be able to survive.

In determining how far business leadership today can properly act in aid of the foreign policy of the government — in aid of the European Recovery Program, for example — we find ourselves in this dilemma. Conditions abroad in many countries are not such as to justify the prudent businessman in embarking on long-term financial commitments. Apart from the inherent risks of war, we have the dollar famine, various forms of foreign governmental measures for the nationalization or domestication of foreign business holdings, and the like. Then there are psychological risks. Many of us remember what happened after the last war when business and bankers, in particular, were castigated for overextending their foreign risks.

When he looks at the devastation in Europe today, the prudent businessman does not have much stomach for venturing into this field. The risks are no longer those of business judgment or acumen; they are basically political or the type of economic risks such as balance of payment or exchange controls which are essentially political in character. If we are to expect American business to go abroad on any substantial scale, there must be some underwriting by the government of the type of risk which today is beyond the control of the businessman. It is time for the representatives of government and of business to get together and analyze the problems which today serve to prevent American business from bringing to bear the full weight of its resources and ingenuity to help toward solving world economic problems. Each side has a very vital interest. Business has a real stake in contributing to the success of our foreign policy. Government also has an interest. It does not, I trust, aspire to continue indefinitely as the world supplier and banker at public expense, and even if a government should wish to do this, the taxpayers would sooner or later bring it to a stop.

The European Recovery Program, China aid, Export-Import Bank loans, and even World Bank loans are necessary as emergency measures for a wounded world. They may be necessary for a considerable time, but they should provide the transition during a recovery period and not the pattern for an indefinite future. And it should be a transition to a time when private business can once more operate abroad without government aid. Unless we start now to study ways and means to encourage private business to work along with government abroad, we are likely to grow into a situation, fateful for our institutions, where government would more and more take over international trade, and business would then tend to lose both the experience and the aptitude for this field of endeavor.

Thus, there is little reality to a discussion in the abstract of the responsibility of business to the world unless we consider at the same time the responsibility which governments may have toward business to make it reasonable for business to venture into the world. If our government is to expect the support of private business in the foreign field under present abnormal conditions, government must help create conditions under which the businessman can operate abroad without risks over and above those which a wise and prudent man entrusted with the money and property of others can be asked to accept.

As we develop a program for world economic revival it is time to determine what practical steps can be taken of mutual benefit to our foreign policy and to business enterprise.

To be concrete, I would suggest the three following subjects for study: first, the provisions in the European Recovery legislation — the Economic Cooperation Act of 1948 — which provide under certain conditions for the guarantee of approved private business ventures; second, the strengthening of measures for the legitimate and more effective protection of business operating abroad; and third, the establishment of more workable machinery as between government and business for the temporary assignment to government duty of business experts with special technical competence.

In the European and China aid plans we have embarked upon the most important business venture in the foreign field that any government has ever undertaken in time of peace. We are proposing to spend over five billion dollars this year and contemplate the possibility of spending an equivalent amount over the three succeeding years to help restore the economy of China and the countries of Western Europe. We are doing this because as a matter of governmental policy we consider this a reasonable investment in the security of the United States. In fact, we are told by those in charge of our military establishment that if we do not do this and if we do not succeed in the ambitious enterprise we have embarked upon, we must look forward to the expenditure of several times these astronomical amounts in increased outlays for our military establishment.

The European Recovery Program, as I have indicated above, has little chance of succeeding unless it is run along business lines and unless sound business principles and management are an essential part of the plan. The Economic Cooperation Act of 1948, which sets up the recovery program, implicitly recognizes that private business cannot be expected at its own cost and expense to bear directly any substantial share of the load, but there are many sections of the act which recognize the need for business participation. In the drafting of the legislation emphasis was placed on the need for business management. The administrator is a businessman and he has gathered around him many men experienced in the business field to represent him here and abroad.

In Section III of the act there is an interesting provision which permits the administrator to use up to three hundred million dollars to guarantee the dollar exchange risk on projects approved by the administrator and by the participating country as furthering the purposes of the act. I understand this provision to mean that American business enterprise can submit to the administrator any type of reconstruction project in any of the European countries covered by the act. If the project is approved and carried out and earns in the local currency of the country an amount sufficient to cover the investment, and if this currency cannot be converted into dollars, then the administrator will take the foreign currency and give the American businessman the equivalent in dollars at the local rate of exchange up to the amount of dollars invested in the project. In this way it is hoped that American business can carry out certain of the projects necessary to European recovery on a private business basis but with certain governmental protection.

Under present abnormal conditions this is a legitimate form of partnership. The government assumes the type of risk which the prudent businessman today cannot be asked to accept when dealing with funds for which he is, in effect, trustee. Thus, there is established a practical method whereby business brains and resourcefulness can contribute to a mutually desirable and important foreign policy objective.

This is pilot legislation in a new field. As such, it is possible that experience will show the need for amendment. Today, business abroad faces not only exchange risks; it faces very real political risks and measures of governmental nationalization as well as the risks of war. If business coöperation is really desired, I see no reason why the guarantee, since it covers only the investment and no profits, should not cover the full range of risks over and above the usual business risks which the businessman would have to meet if he were investing his money in the United States.

Government and business should get together and work out a feasible program along these lines so that it may be possible to get business know-how back of the foreign recovery program.

A second field for possible exploration between government and business, to make it practicable for American business to engage more seriously in the foreign field, is that of the protection to be accorded American foreign investments.

The plan of guarantee discussed above relates only to the Marshall-Plan countries. Further, it is a temporary measure. There are many other countries of the world where American business is hesitant to enter because of the long history of measures of governmental expropriation and discrimination, and because of the present growing fear of government nationalization. There have been far too many instances where American investments abroad have been wiped out by government action and no effective reparation made.

I do not suggest for a minute that we should return to the days of dollar diplomacy or to the era when business asked for battleships. That has properly gone forever and with it the days of colonial exploitation. But the measures of protection for American business abroad have not been overhauled or reviewed for decades. They are completely archaic and unrealistic. In particular, our policy has not been reconsidered in the light of the American position as the world's banker and economic arsenal. Mere diplomatic representation on behalf of American interests and the usual advice to claimants to exhaust their legal remedies in the local courts in many countries of the world result only in exhausting the harried businessman.

I do not suggest that we replace dollar diplomacy by some form of economic imperialism or turn the economic powers we enjoy today into weapons of reprisal. We could, however, properly use our economic position to help work out a generally accepted code of fair dealing which would apply in all countries to the protection of foreign business enterprise. Even our own country is not entirely blameless. We have gone very far in certain wartime legislation in taking over property of foreigners other than that of enemy nationals.

If justice is to be done, it may be necessary to establish an international tribunal to pass upon and determine legal rights in all cases where as the result of governmental action the property interests of foreigners have been damaged and no adequate compensation made. Today there exists no such tribunal with competence to deal with these matters. Recourse to the tribunal could be limited to instances where the government of the aggrieved national was prepared to recommend the case to the international tribunal as one meriting its consideration. If such an impartial tribunal rendered its decision and the decision was not respected, then any action which a country like the United States might take through exercise of its economic power would be in support of an international decision and not a unilateral effort to protect its own nationals.

If in this way we could get away from the musty and ineffective precedents of the past, as well as from the taint of dollar diplomacy or economic imperialism, we might create a far more solid basis for encouraging American business to assume the risk of venturing abroad. In this way, too, business would be encouraged on its own initiative to supplement the program of foreign aid which is one of the cornerstones today of our foreign policy.

Finally, there is the question of aiding government to obtain competent personnel on a temporary basis to help it meet certain of its economic responsibilities abroad. As long as our government is in the field of international business and banking on the scale that now prevails, government must do one of two things: either build up its own foreign civil service, or borrow competent personnel from the outside.

Today, to meet the temporary emergency, men are being borrowed from business and the professions. Many corporations and firms have shown a high degree of patriotism in releasing their men to government for this essential service. To my mind, this is a sacrifice that business on a voluntary basis can and should make. But the conditions of such service are ill-defined and in many cases unsatisfactory. We have had our dollar-a-year men and various other haphazard arrangements. In many cases the conditions imposed under civil service are too restrictive and are ill adapted to the type of men and to the nature of the services to be rendered. In some cases businesses have been subject to wholly unfair criticism when, after lending men to the government at substantial sacrifice, they have been accused, generally I believe wholly unjustly, of planting men in official positions in order to render service to their private companies.

It has been suggested that, following the British pattern, we should develop something in the nature of an overseas civil service to supplement our organized

Foreign Service. Today we do not have the time, even if we should have the desire, to create an adequate civil service to meet the business needs of government in the foreign field. In fact, I doubt whether we could ever meet these needs adequately through a civil service. Highly skilled specialists are required for particular jobs, often for a limited period. No civil service can provide such men, and over a long period there would probably not be sufficient demand or sufficient opportunities to justify the creation of a special business foreign civil service or to attract the high quality of man such a service requires.

Here again a great service could be rendered if government and business could work out a plan, and implement it with legislation, whereby business on a voluntary basis and under fair conditions would accept the sacrifice incident to making available appropriate personnel for temporary employment by government as long as government perforce remains in the business field abroad. The administrator for the European Recovery Program has, I understand, over thirty thousand applicants for jobs. It is questionable whether any substantial percentage of these applicants are really qualified and the task of sorting them out is like finding the needle in the haystack. Here is a case where the job should seek the man. Only business and the professions can furnish the proper personnel.

To conclude, American responsibility abroad can be met only if American business maintains a strong and free economy here at home. And in the foreign field, to secure the effective coöperation of American business there must be a realistic reappraisal of the relations between government and business in the great undertakings forced upon government by the breakdown through war of the economic life of half a world.

Bei Fragen zur Produktsicherheit wenden Sie sich bitte an:
If you have any questions regarding product safety,
please contact:

Walter de Gruyter GmbH
Genthiner Straße 13
10785 Berlin
productsafety@degruyterbrill.com